D0838526

BACKYARD WILDLIFE

Chipmunks

by Derek Zobel

BLASTOFF! READERS

BELLWETHER MEDIA · MINNEAPOLIS, MN

Note to Librarians, Teachers, and Parents:

Blastoff! Readers are carefully developed by literacy experts and combine standards-based content with developmentally appropriate text.

Level 1 provides the most support through repetition of high-frequency words, light text, predictable sentence patterns, and strong visual support.

Level 2 offers early readers a bit more challenge through varied simple sentences, increased text load, and less repetition of high-frequency words.

Level 3 advances early-fluent readers toward fluency through increased text and concept load, less reliance on visuals, longer sentences, and more literary language.

Level 4 builds reading stamina by providing more text per page, increased use of punctuation, greater variation in sentence patterns, and increasingly challenging vocabulary.

Level 5 encourages children to move from "learning to read" to "reading to learn" by providing even more text, varied writing styles, and less familiar topics.

Whichever book is right for your reader, Blastoff! Readers are the perfect books to build confidence and encourage a love of reading that will last a lifetime!

This edition first published in 2011 by Bellwether Media, Inc.

No part of this publication may be reproduced in whole or in part without written permission of the publisher. For information regarding permission, write to Bellwether Media, Inc., Attention: Permissions Department, 5357 Penn Avenue South, Minneapolis, MN 55419.

Library of Congress Cataloging-in-Publication Data
Zobel, Derek, 1983–
  Chipmunks / by Derek Zobel.
     p. cm. – (Blastoff! readers. Backyard wildlife)
  Summary: "Developed by literacy experts for students in kindergarten through grade three, this book introduces chipmunks to young readers through leveled text and related photos"–Provided by publisher.
  Includes bibliographical references and index.
  ISBN 978-1-60014-438-7 (hardcover : alk. paper)   H385 066 7   11/10
  1. Chipmunks–Juvenile literature. I. Title.
  QL737.R68Z63 2011
  599.36'4–dc22   2010010560

Text copyright © 2011 by Bellwether Media, Inc. BLASTOFF! READERS and associated logos are trademarks and/or registered trademarks of Bellwether Media, Inc.

Printed in the United States of America, North Mankato, MN.

080110   1162

Contents

Chipmunks are **rodents** with stripes. They live in grasslands, forests, and deserts.

Chipmunks are named for the *chip* sound that they make.

Chipmunks have bushy tails. Their tails help them **balance** in trees.

Claws help chipmunks grip tree trunks and branches.

Chipmunks also use their claws to dig **burrows**.

Chipmunks eat fruits, nuts, grains, and **insects**.

Chipmunks have **pouches** in their cheeks. They store food in them.

Chipmunks push
on their full cheeks
to get food out.

Chipmunks **hibernate** in the winter. They wake up to eat in the spring. Time to search for food!

Glossary

balance—to stay steady and not fall

burrows—tunnels chipmunks dig; chipmunks live in burrows.

claws—nails on the feet of chipmunks; claws help chipmunks climb and dig.

hibernate—to sleep through the winter

insects—small animals with six legs and hard outer bodies; insect bodies are divided into three parts.

pouches—pockets some animals use to store things; chipmunks have pouches in their cheeks to store food.

rodents—a group of small animals that usually gnaw, or nibble, on their food

To Learn More

AT THE LIBRARY

Bastian, Lois Brunner. *Chipmunk Family*. New York, N.Y.: Franklin Watts, 2000.

Miller, Kathy M. *Chippy Chipmunk Parties in the Garden*. New Ringgold, Penn.: Celtic Sunrise, 2009.

Whitehouse, Patricia. *Chipmunks*. Chicago, Ill.: Heinemann Library, 2004.

ON THE WEB

Learning more about chipmunks is as easy as 1, 2, 3.

1. Go to www.factsurfer.com.

2. Enter "chipmunks" into the search box.

3. Click the "Surf" button and you will see a list of related Web sites.

With factsurfer.com, finding more information is just a click away.

Index

The images in this book are reproduced through the courtesy of: Juan Martinez, front cover, pp. 5 (left, middle), 15 (right), 19, 21; John Cancalosi/Photolibrary, p. 5; John R. McNair, p. 5 (right); Margaret M. Stewart, pp. 7, 9, 17; Kateryna Dyellalova, p. 11; Frank Cezus/Getty Images, p. 13; Juniors Bildarchiv/Photolibrary, p. 15; Martin Novak, p. 15 (left); Kai Wong, p. 15 (middle).